AF316706

This book is dedicated to Dr. Arthur E. "Buck" Rikli (1917-2015),
whose many years of dedicated research of the ancestors of
Abraham Friedrich Rikli (1795-1866) and Verena Moser-Rikli (1798-1868)
of Wangen, Switzerland, made this book possible.

STARS IN THE SKY
A Story of the Rikli Family History

Copyright @ 2022 by Tamara Choat and Gloria Rikli Choat
Illustrations by 'Art by Niaz' and Marta Morgan

All rights reserved. No part of this book may be
reproduced or transmitted in any form or by any
means without written permission from the author.

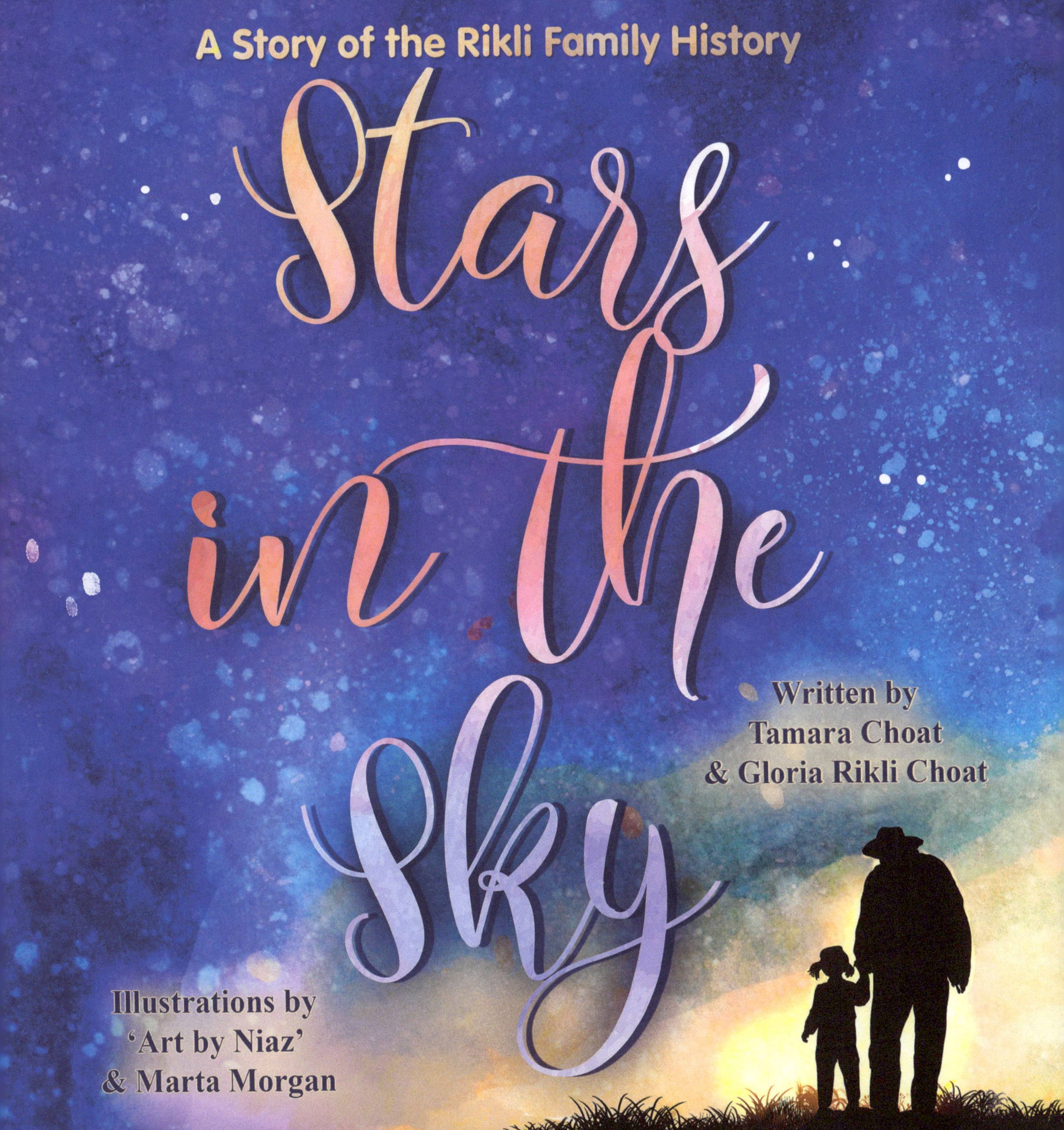
A Story of the Rikli Family History
Stars in the sky
Written by
Tamara Choat
& Gloria Rikli Choat
Illustrations by
'Art by Niaz'
& Marta Morgan

"Grandfather...

Grandfather...???"
said Margaret, as she
stumbled sleepily into the
room. "Are you still awake?"

"Sweet Margaret ... what are you
doing still awake?"

"I ... I just keep thinking about seeing
all my aunts and uncles and cousins
tomorrow, and playing softball,
and singing ... and I'm just too
excited to sleep."

"Let's ask Grandmother for a cup of warm milk, and I'll tell you a story," said Grandfather, as Margaret climbed onto his lap.

"This is a story about the reason we gather for reunions, to remember and cherish our family.

"It begins with your great-great-great grandfather, Arnold Rikli. Or, as they say in Switzerland, where he was born in 1823, your 'ur-ur-ur-grossvater'!

"Arnold's parents were Abraham Friedrich and Verena Moser-Rikli, who lived in Wangen an der Aare."

"What? They lived in a wagon in the air?"

"No," said Grandfather, chuckling. "That was the name of their town in a country called Switzerland. The Rikli family had lived here for over 500 years."

"Wow ... 500 years," said Margaret. "Is that how old you are Grandfather?"

Grandfather laughed.

"Well, not quite, Margaret. Although sometimes I feel it! I could use some of Arnold's naturopathic treatments!"

"A nature-path? Did he walk on a trail in the forest to feel better?" asked Margaret.

"Well, not quite, but it was kind of like that," said Grandfather. "Let me tell you about him."

"Arnold's father was a very successful man who owned a red-dye factory. The Rikli factory was famous for a unique color they called 'Turkish red.' They shipped this dye all over the world.

"A plant called 'madder root' was used to make the red color. But the madder root didn't always work right and sometimes the yarn wouldn't turn the right color. This caused a lot of yarn to be ruined and they lost a lot of money."

Margaret giggled. "That would make me madder and madder and MADDER too!"

Grandfather laughed.

"Actually," he said, "Abraham relied on his deep faith in God to overcome hard times. Even though he was rich and could have hired caregivers for his children, like many people did back then, Abraham believed parents give their children the best care.

"He said, 'How could I hire a stranger and possibly endanger the clean souls of my children, who are worth more to me than the treasures of this world?'"

"It was in this household of family love and faith in God that little Arnold was raised with his ten brothers and sisters."

Margaret sipped on her warm milk, then yawned as she snuggled on Grandfather's lap.

"Close your eyes, Margaret," said Grandfather,
"and picture this story I'm going to tell you
about Arnold Rikli as a boy."

"Young Arnold was high-spirited and had a great love for the outdoors. He loved playing in the creek that ran past his father's dye factory. He would sit on the banks and soak up the sun, or jump in the creek and let the water flow over him.

"Arnold believed being outside was the most wonderful thing possible. He studied as much about nature as he could in the beautiful outdoors of Switzerland.

"He noticed plants and animals thrived when they had lots of sunshine, water and air. He believed people would do the same."

"As Arnold grew older he traveled across Europe and studied to be a doctor — but a different kind of doctor than most. His passion was to find ways to heal people with sunshine, water and air.

"Dr. Rikli's methods worked well, but some people doubted him because his ways were different.

"Eventually, he helped heal so many that people began to believe him.

"Especially after a very sad event."

"What happened?" asked
Margaret, suddenly wide awake.

"One day," said Grandfather, "Arnold, or Dr. Rikli, as he was now called, was standing near a flooded stream with fast whirlpools. He saw a man fall in and go under the water. Arnold dove into the dangerous, muddy water to try and save him. Three other men dove in to help.

"But the water swirled and sucked all of them under the current.

"Arnold tried his best to save the men, but the water was too fast and too deep."

"Time ticked by.

"The people watching were horrified."

"Eventually the water swirled upward and out emerged Arnold. As a child Arnold had practiced diving in the creek he loved and learned to hold his breath for a very long time."

"Arnold lived only because he knew how to swim and hold his breath so well. The people on the shore said he had been underwater for three minutes — almost an eternity — without taking a breath.

"Sadly, all three of the other men died that day. Arnold was sorrowful about that his entire life."

"That's a really sad story," said Margaret, "But I'm glad Arnold survived so he could become my ur-ur-ur grossvater!"

"That's right. It was all a part of God's plan," said Grandfather. "Do you want to hear more of the story?"

"Yes I do!" said Margaret.

"Arnold moved to Austria, where his father wanted him to build another red dye factory. But the chemicals in the dye made Arnold very sick. He used his methods of sunshine, water and air to heal himself, but decided he didn't want to work in the dye business anymore.

"So he started a natural healing center near Lake Bled in Slovenia. His treatments included swimming in thermal water, sun tanning and walking. He is still famous today for being a founder of natural healing."

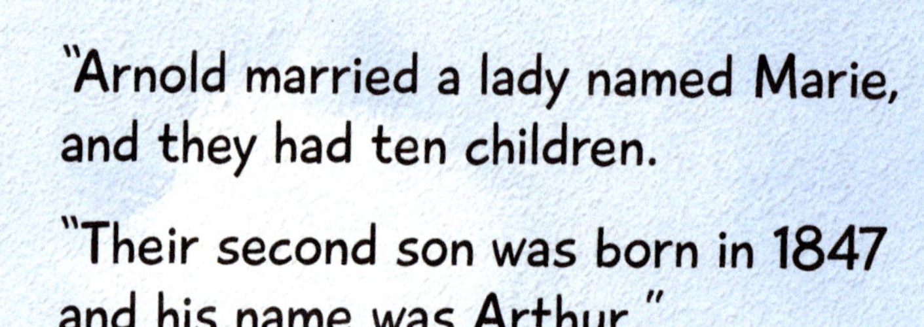

"Arnold married a lady named Marie, and they had ten children.

"Their second son was born in 1847 and his name was Arthur."

"Now, Arthur loved Austria, but he felt there was adventure in the new land of America. So when he was 19 years old he said goodbye to his family and sailed to America. Arthur first lived in Wisconsin and then moved to Nebraska. Here he fell in love with and married Margaretta."

"Do you mean Margaret, like me?" asked Margaret.

"No, her name was actually Margaretta. It was a German name, because she had been born in Germany. I think maybe your parents had Margaretta in mind when they named you," said Grandfather. Arthur and Margaretta had 12 children!"

"That's a lot of kids!" said Margaret.

"Maybe that's why he became a farmer, to feed everyone!" said Grandfather. "He first owned a hardware store, then bought a farm near a little town called Murdock."

"Is that the farm we are going to visit at the family reunion?" asked Margaret.

"Yes, we'll see the old barn painted with the Rikli family crest," said Grandfather. "The house Arthur built and raised his family in stood right beside it for years, and inside was a portrait of — guess who?"

"Arnold? The doctor?" exclaimed Margaret.

"That's right," said Grandfather. "Dr. Rikli who loved sunshine, water and air. His legacy and his faith in God passed down through his family, many who are also doctors, businessmen and farmers. They too depend on sunshine, water and air, but, most importantly, faith in God, to help their crops and families grow."

"So all of us at the reunion are related to Grandfather Arthur and Grandma Margaretta?" asked Margaret.

"That's right, we are all related. And not just by blood, but also by our faith in God."

"Grandfather ... do you know what I think?" asked Margaret.

"Do you remember Abraham in the Bible? And how God promised him that one day he would have as many descendants as there are stars in the sky?"

"Of course I do," said Grandfather.

"I think that God blessed Abraham Rikli just like he did Abraham in the Bible. Our family has had faith in God, and he has protected us and kept us together."

Grandfather smiled at Margaret.

"Yes, Margaret. I think you are right. God has blessed us richly," he said.

"Now Little Miss Rikli, go get some sleep so you can play with your cousins tomorrow."

stars
in the
sky

Dear Reader:

I want to thank my very talented daughter-in-love, Tamara Choat for writing this story 14 years ago as a puppet skit for our Rikli Reunion talent show. It was her suggestion we turn this story into a children's book as our reunion came to a close in 2018. Our numbers were dwindling, and we feared our rich history would soon be lost. Through the encouragement and financial donations from many Rikli family members, the idea began to take shape and finally has become a reality. Tamara is married to my son, Travis, and they farm and ranch near Terry, Montana. She received her bachelor's degree in agricultural communications and master's degree in international studies at Oklahoma State University, where she met my son. After the birth of their fourth child, it was decided I would jump in to help complete the project. It has been a true labor of love.

Thank you to Charles Rikli, grandson of William and Marie Rikli and Michael Gregory (deceased), grandson of Emma Rikli Gregory. Charles spent many hours gathering, scanning and uploading photos and documents to our family website, www.RikliFamily.com. Michael devoted a great deal of his time to maintaining and updating the work of Arthur (Buck) Rikli in mapping our genealogy. This information was invaluable to Tamara and me in completing this book. Please take time to visit the website. In addition to many more photos and documents, you will find a Descendancy Chart (the most current to my knowledge) and hopefully you can find where you fit in. We welcome your comments and updates to the family tree via email to RikliReunion@hotmail.com.

I owe a debt of gratitude to my father, Oliver Rikli, son of Oscar and Hazel Rikli, who instilled in me a great love of family, and to my sisters, Chris, and Evelyn for encouraging me to finish this book. We always looked forward to attending our Rikli Reunions every two years while we were growing up. I have fond memories of listening to the Rikli Quartet (Roland, Mark, Vernon, and Dutch Rikli), and watching my dad, Oliver, and my uncle, Carol, present their interpretation of the famous poem, "Casey at the Bat". It is my hope and prayer this book will help keep the candle burning so our children and grandchildren will pass on the family legacy for many years to come.

Although great care was taken to present the information available to us and to represent all surviving members of the Arthur Rikli family as accurately as possible, we know it is not without error. We ask you to accept this story in the spirit it was intended and overlook any shortcomings. We hope you and your children enjoy this story of our Rikli family.

Gloria Rikli Choat, Co-Author

Arthur Rikli family, circa 1898
Front: Arnold, Grandpa Arthur, Leo, Grandma Margaretta (Oehl), Lorenz (never married)
Center: Albert, William, Emil
Back Row: Emma, Mary Helena, Arthur, Elizabeth, Oscar
Not pictured: Alfred (1873-1881)

Arnold and Martha Oehme Rikli
wedding photo. 9 children; 2F, 7M

Grandma Margaretta with Elsie and
Walter, two of Arnold's children

Arthur Richard Rikli
Spouse: Sarah Brown
4 children; 3F, 1M

Arthur's wife, Sarah Brown Rikli

Mary Helena Rikli Stolz
Spouse: Walter Stolz. 3 children; 2F, 1M

Margaret Elizabeth (Lizzie) Rikli
Spouse: Fredrick (Curt) Opitz. 7 children; 7M

Front: Curt Opitz and Lizzie Rikli Opitz (25th Anniversary)
Center: Luther, Albert, Emil   Back: Curtie, Arthur, Oscar (Skeet), Martin

Emma Rikli Gregory
Spouse: Walter Cowan Gregory
8 children; 3F, 5M

Walter and Emma Rikli Gregory wedding photo

Hazel Oliver Rikli and Oscar Rikli wedding photo
3 children; 2M, 1F

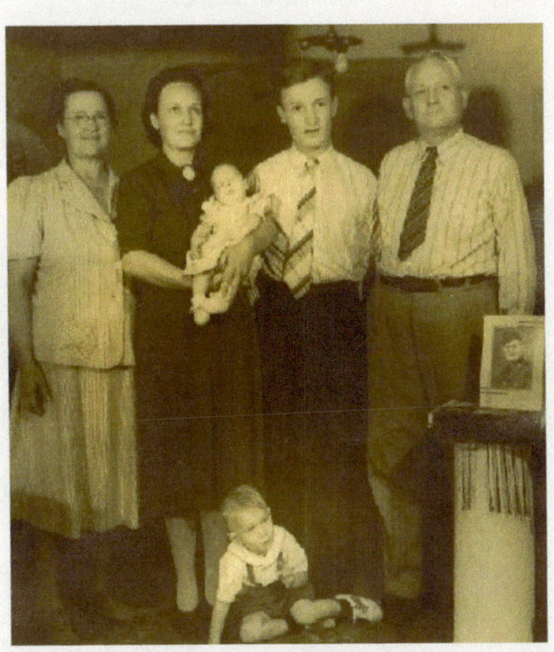

Hazel, Kathryn Rikli Taggart with Terry, Carol,
Oscar, Oliver in army photo; Floor: Tim Taggart

William Edward and Marie Merkle Rikli
wedding photo. 4 children; 1F, 3M

Front: Will, Marcus, Marie
Back: Bernice Rikli Kuehn, Roland, Alfred

Emil and Bertha Nolting Rikli wedding photo
3 children; 2F, 1M (with Albert and Bessie)

Albert and Bessie Bracken Rikli wedding photo
5 children; 3F, 2M

Leo Roland and Edna Johannsen Rikli
wedding photo. 4 children; 1F, 3M

Front: Edna, Leo
Back: Naomi, Warren (Abe), Vernon, Donald (Dutch)

Five Rikli brothers, 1902
Front: Oscar, William   Back: Leo, Albert, Emil

Twins Albert and Emil Rikli

Will Rikli, Charlie R. (neighbor) and Oscar Rikli

Family photo taken at 50th wedding anniversary celebration of Arthur and Margaretta with eleven surviving siblings. In background is the original homestead where the children were raised near Murdock, Nebraska (1920).

Onneatta and Dutch Rikli (youngest son of Leo Rikli) with Nebraska Pioneer Farm Award for 100 years of continuous family ownership of the Arthur and Margaretta Rikli farmstead.

www.ingramcontent.com/pod-product-compliance
Lightning Source LLC
Chambersburg PA
CBHW042324140726
48196CB00016B/715